BLACK
HAIR

BLACK HAIR

GARY SOTO

UNIVERSITY OF
PITTSBURGH
PRESS

Published by the University of Pittsburgh Press, Pittsburgh, Pa. 15260
Copyright © 1985, Gary Soto
Feffer and Simons, Inc., London
Manufactured in the United States of America

Library of Congress Cataloging in Publication Data

Soto, Gary.
  Black hair.

  (Pitt poetry series)
   I. Title.   II. Series.
PS3569.072B5   1985   811'.54   84-5184
ISBN 0-8229-3498-1
ISBN 0-8229-5362-5 (pbk.)

Some of these poems originally appeared in the following periodicals: *The American Poetry Review, Crazyhorse, The Missouri Review, Open Places, Poetry NOW, Revista Chicano-Requena,* and *The Three Penny Review.* "Ode to the Yard Sale" was originally published in *Telescope* and copyrighted by The Galileo Press. "Ambition," "Between Words," "Desire," "Envying the Children of San Francisco," "The Estonian Comes to Dinner," "Failing in the Presence of Ants," "Finding a Lucky Number," "Getting Serious," "Hunger Among Crabs," "The Jungle Cafe," "Looking Around, Believing," "Morning on This Street," "Oranges," "The Plum's Heart," "Saturday Under the Sky," and "When We Wake" first appeared in *Poetry,* copyrighted 1982, 1983, and 1984 by the Modern Poetry Association, and are reprinted by permission of the editor of *Poetry.*

The author wishes to thank Christopher Buckley, Leonard Nathan, and his wife Carolyn for first looking at these poems.

The publication of this book is supported by grants from the National Endowment for the Arts in Washington, D.C., a Federal agency, and the Pennsylvania Council on the Arts.

for Carolyn and Mariko

CONTENTS

CONTENTS

1

ONE

BLACK HAIR

At eight I was brilliant with my body.
In July, that ring of heat
We all jumped through, I sat in the bleachers
Of Romain Playground, in the lengthening
Shade that rose from our dirty feet.
The game before us was more than baseball.
It was a figure—Hector Moreno
Quick and hard with turned muscles,
His crouch the one I assumed before an altar
Of worn baseball cards, in my room.

I came here because I was Mexican, a stick
Of brown light in love with those
Who could do it—the triple and hard slide,
The gloves eating balls into double plays.
What could I do with 50 pounds, my shyness,
My black torch of hair, about to go out?
Father was dead, his face no longer
Hanging over the table or our sleep,
And mother was the terror of mouths
Twisting hurt by butter knives.

In the bleachers I was brilliant with my body,
Waving players in and stomping my feet,
Growing sweaty in the presence of white shirts.
I chewed sunflower seeds. I drank water
And bit my arm through the late innings.
When Hector lined balls into deep
Center, in my mind I rounded the bases
With him, my face flared, my hair lifting
Beautifully, because we were coming home
To the arms of brown people.

IN AUGUST

A blimp was above me
And then gone,
Like all I would ever know.
Like father with hands in my hair.
Like uncle on the porch with his arms
And little else. I walked
In the alley looking up
Until it wasn't the sky before
Me, but a plum tree,
Its dark fruit, notched and open
Where birds ate. I climbed
Into it, searched, dropped
With two in each hand.
I walked from the alley
To Coleman Pickle
Where brother, friends, tiny sister
Were standing in barrels,
Pickles in their hands
And saying, they're good,
Better than plums. I climbed
Into a barrel and fished for one
—came up to see the blimp
Pass quietly as a cloud,
Its shadow dark enough to sleep
Or dream in. We watched
It, with food in our mouths,
All wondering, until it was above us
And then gone,
Like all we would ever know.

THE PLUM'S HEART

I've climbed in trees
To eat, and climbed
Down to look about
This world, mouth red
From plums that were
Once clouds in March
—rain I mean, that
Pitiless noise against
Leaves and branches.
Father once lifted me
Into one, and from
A distance I might
Have been a limb,
Moving a little heavier
Than most but a limb
All the same. My hands
Opened like mouths,
The juice running
Without course down
My arms, as I stabbed
For plums, bunched
Or half-hidden behind
Leaves. A bird fluttered
From there, a single
Leaf cutting loose,
And gnats like smoke
Around a bruised plum.
I climbed searching
For those red globes,
And with a sack filled,

I called for father
To catch—father
Who would disappear
Like fruit at the end
Of summer, from a neck
Wound some say—blood
Running like the juice
Of these arms. I
Twisted the throat
Of the sack, tossed
It, and started down
To father, his mouth
Already red and grinning
Like the dead on their
Rack of blackness.
When I jumped, he was
Calling, arms open,
The sack at his feet
For us, the half-bitten,
Who bring on the flies.

ORANGES

The first time I walked
With a girl, I was twelve,
Cold, and weighted down
With two oranges in my jacket.
December. Frost cracking
Beneath my steps, my breath
Before me, then gone,
As I walked toward
Her house, the one whose
Porch light burned yellow
Night and day, in any weather.
A dog barked at me, until
She came out pulling
At her gloves, face bright
With rouge. I smiled,
Touched her shoulder, and led
Her down the street, across
A used car lot and a line
Of newly planted trees,
Until we were breathing
Before a drugstore. We
Entered, the tiny bell
Bringing a saleslady
Down a narrow aisle of goods.
I turned to the candies
Tiered like bleachers,
And asked what she wanted—
Light in her eyes, a smile
Starting at the corners
Of her mouth. I fingered
A nickel in my pocket,

And when she lifted a chocolate
That cost a dime,
I didn't say anything.
I took the nickel from
My pocket, then an orange,
And set them quietly on
The counter. When I looked up,
The lady's eyes met mine,
And held them, knowing
Very well what it was all
About.

Outside,
A few cars hissing past,
Fog hanging like old
Coats between the trees.
I took my girl's hand
In mine for two blocks,
Then released it to let
Her unwrap the chocolate.
I peeled my orange
That was so bright against
The gray of December
That, from some distance,
Someone might have thought
I was making a fire in my hands.

WHO ARE YOU?

Once, when a tiny man in a suit
Fell, I raced down the stairs into the street
To lift him like a chair, in the early
Dusk, in the glory of my muscles,
Of my mind that was clear as rain on leaves.
I lifted him and asked how he was.
He answered, What are you? Italian?
No, Mexican, I told him, and he asked, Jewish?
No, No! Mexican, and I pointed to my wrist.
He smacked his lips; wiped his brow.
This elf of a man with the beard
Of a topnotch goat, said he knew
What I meant, waved, but turned back
To ask: Is that your place?
He pointed to my house—
The running kids, a grandfather
With a paint bucket, the gray laundry
Waving like flags on the line.
I know who you are, he told me, and turned
Away, with a soft Thank You, thank you.

9

THE DAY AFTER

to F. G.

My brother says you came back
And were at the foot of his bed,
Green and telling him it was OK,
The darkness, the place where
You sit, waiting for this country
To turn with flames. I'm waiting,
Too, for the flash from a mirror,
A voice from the other end
Saying it's over—things fall from
The sky in an applause
Of ash, brick over red brick.
We may die over a sandwich, between
Phone calls, and not know we've missed it,
The bloom of smoke and the bones
Lit under running flesh.
I'm waiting for this day, and for you,
Frank, to show yourself, green
Or any other way—to tell me
It's OK, that I can shake
Off my sins and begin again, a child
Among many. In that world
If I pressed my face to a fogged
Window, I wouldn't know what goes on.
A wipe of the sleeve, and it's new again.

10

LANDSCAPE IN SPRING

In a pickup my brother and me,
And some fat guy, are drinking from paper bags,
Our necks blackened, our hair loose in wind.
We're two thousand years from Jesus
And the foothills, saints, dogs running
In rain, Paris, women in Paris . . .
To the left, a Mexican waving us down with a hat.
To the right, a burst of tractor smoke
Coming apart, and a single house,
White and grumbling in the heat—
A woman in the yard with a hose pointed
At a tree. But we're not stopping,
And that house is going to stay
Where it is. We're speeding
Through the day, and if we're pointed
To a field, cotton or beet, we'll cut it
With a hoe. Good pay, bad pay,
It's all the same if you're brown
And given hours to think about the sun.
Work in dust, get up in dust. Beer makes it go.

IN THE MADNESS OF LOVE

Richard on the cold roof screams, I'm the eye
Of Omar, and a friend and I, with crumbs
Falling from our mouths, shout for him to get
Down, to remember that the rent is due
And it's no time to act silly.
Look, he says, and we look: a burst
Of sparrows. No, the clouds, he says,
They are coming. We plead with raisins,
Watery plums, but he's distant as the sky—
Dark with kites crossing over to rain.
We plead with a sandwich, car keys, albums;
Threaten him with a hose, our black neighbor
The drummer. No use. I climb on all fours
Over the roof, unsteady as a wobbly chair,
And when I touch him he shivers
Like a kicked dog. I take hold and rock him
In my arms, his jaw stiff with rage
And his eyes so wet we could drink from them
And be free. What is it? I ask.
There, he points. And the clouds begin to move.

CRUEL BOYS

First day. Jackie and I walking in leaves
On our way to becoming 8th graders,
Pencils behind our ears, pee-chee folders
Already scribbled with football players
In dresses, track star in a drooped bra.
We're tough. I'm Mexican
And he's an unkillable Okie with three
Teeth in his pocket, sludge under
His nails from scratching oily pants.
No one's going to break us, not the dean
Or principal, not the cops
Who could arrive in pairs, walkie-talkies
To their mouths, warning:
"Dangerous. They have footballs."
We could bounce them off their heads
And reporters might show up
With shirt sleeves rolled up to their ears,
Asking our age, if we're Catholic.
But this never happens. We go to first
Period, math, then second period, geography,
And in third period, English, the woman
Teacher reads us Frost, something
About a tree, and to set things straight,
How each day will fall like a tree.
Jackie raises his hand, stands up,
And shouts, "You ain't nothing but a hound dog,"
As the spitballs begin to fly.

BEHIND GRANDMA'S HOUSE

At ten I wanted fame. I had a comb
And two Coke bottles, a tube of Bryl-creem.
I borrowed a dog, one with
Mismatched eyes and a happy tongue,
And wanted to prove I was tough
In the alley, kicking over trash cans,
A dull chime of tuna cans falling.
I hurled light bulbs like grenades
And men teachers held their heads,
Fingers of blood lengthening
On the ground. I flicked rocks at cats,
Their goofy faces spurred with foxtails.
I kicked fences. I shooed pigeons.
I broke a branch from a flowering peach
And frightened ants with a stream of piss.
I said "Shit," "Fuck you," and "No way
Daddy-O" to an imaginary priest
Until grandma came into the alley,
Her apron flapping in a breeze,
Her hair mussed, and said, "Let me help you,"
And punched me between the eyes.

BROWN GIRL, BLONDE OKIE

Jackie and I cross-legged
In the yard, plucking at
Grass, cupping flies
And shattering them against
Each other's faces—
Smiling that it's summer,
No school, and we can
Sleep out under stars
And the blink of jets
Crossing up our lives.
The flies leave, or die,
And we are in the dark,
Still cross-legged,
Talking not dogs or baseball,
But whom will we love,
What brown girl or blonde
Okie to open up to
And say we are sorry
For our faces, the filth
We shake from our hair,
The teeth without direction.
"We're ugly," says Jackie
On one elbow, and stares
Lost between jets
At what this might mean.
In the dark I touch my
Nose, trace my lips, and pinch
My mouth into a dull flower.
Oh God, we're in trouble.

LEARNING TO BARGAIN

Summer. Flies knitting
Filth on the window,
A mother calling a son home . . .
I'm at that window, looking
Onto the street: dusk,
A neighbor kid sharpening
A stick at the curb.
I go outside and sit
Next to him without saying
A word. When he looks
Up, his eyes dark as flies . . .
I ask about the cat, the one dead
Among weeds in the alley.
"Yeah, I did it," he admits,
And stares down at his feet,
Then my feet. "What do you want?"
"A dime," I say. Without
Looking at me, he gets
Up, goes behind his house,
And returns with two Coke bottles.
"These make a dime." He sits
At the curb, his shoulders
So bony they could be wings
To lift him so far. "Don't tell."
He snaps a candy into halves
And we eat in silence.

BEING HUMAN

Jackie asked, Should we? I smiled,
Is God looking? We hunched our shoulders
Like birds in overcoats, and started
Kicking a Republican's fence,
The pickets working loose, some cracking
Like fire under an eager wind.
We stood back, eyeing what we had done,
And kicked in a few more for good
Measure, and then started down the street,
Jackie sucking at a sliver in his palm,
Me whistling "If I Had a Hammer,"
Our cheeks red enough to get
Us through a cold day.
                                                    We looked
Healthy, the children of Dutch paintings.
If some grandpa had opened his curtain
To the morning as we passed
He might have eased into his chair, coffee
Cup in hand, and thought that things
Were not so bad, that the world
Was not falling apart like an old fence,
That there were young people walking
Shoulder to shoulder, in step,
One looking about in wonder, the other
With a song that was endlessly good.

IN OUR PLACE

Johnny, bad boy
Of this street,
That alley,
Friend to me
Under any cloud,
The sea must
Have been inside
You, or why the curly
Hair, the salt
Of shoulders,
The wind, you
And your pockets
Of keys, wood,
Marbles, burnt
Matches—the sea
Will give them up
In time. We ran
Until we looked
Like the sea,
Wet and glinting,
But rose higher
Into trees—fruit
In our mouths
And fingers sticky
As jars,
As the past
That won't let go.
We ate, talked,

And jumped down
Into the alley,
The grasses like
Tiny locks
At our ankles,
And raced yellow
Flowers into blossom.

Last week I dreamed
You. Yesterday
I was on the old
Street, many
Of the houses gone
To simple dust
—though I stopped
At one yard:
A grandmother I knew
And you knew.
She remembered us
With her oranges
In our hands
And how she chased
Us from the yard;
Remembered Andrea
And Sue, the neighbors
With two kids, three
Kids, or none;

Remembered trees,
Cars up on blocks,
Those who ate
And those who didn't
—even dogs
Who walked slow
As tired mailmen;
Remembered until
She went quiet
As water, dreamy
And staring at the grass
At her feet,
And for a moment
She looked like
My mother, your mother,
Tired of these days
And the ones gone,
Her face like
A hurt bird
On her shoulders.
She sighed, looked up,
And said, Honey,
How is it with you?

THE STREET AS FRONTIER

In this good life
I can get up
On my own, eat,
Stand on the floor
Furnace, hair
Flicking about
And eager to
Get down the street,
That torn sheet
Of fog I can step
Through and hurry
Back with oranges—
Princely fruit,
Nugget of juice
For the talking hands
Of the poor.
I put on a shirt,
Shoes. The
House is quiet:
Brother in bed,
Our dog like a dropped
Coat on the floor,
Except breathing.
I leave and take
My place in it all—
Fire in the gutter,
Kids, gray men
Stirring trash
With a stick:
Their long coats
Are the beards
Of the ever wisest.

My coat falls
To my waist.
It's trouble
I want—old girl,
New girl, fired-up
Bush to chase me
Up the street,
Back down, and up again.
One step, two step,
Hand over crazy hand,
And at twenty
I can have it all.

HEAVEN

Scott and I bent
To the radio, legs
Twitching to The Stones,
Faces wet, arms rising
And falling as if
Trying to get out or
Crawl the air—the
Air thick with our
Toweled smells.

                    It's
'64, and our room
And its shaft of dust,
Turning, is all
There is—though Mamma
Says there's the car
To wash, the weeds,
The grass and garbage
Tilting on the back steps.
"Yeh, yeh," we scream
Behind the closed door,
And boost the radio
To "10" and begin
Bouncing on the bed,
Singing, making up
Words about this girl,
That car, tears,
Lipstick, handjives
In alleys—bouncing
Hard, legs split, arms
Open for the Lord,

Until Scott can't stand it
And crashes through
The screened window
And tumbles into a bush,
His shoulders locked
Between branches,
His forehead scratched,
But still singing,
"Baby, baby, o baby."

HOW TO SELL THINGS

for Omar

First, you need a dog
Chased hungry by a cloud
All night, fur over
His eyes, breath white
In the early morning
That has sent you door
To door with a sack
Of oranges. Two for
A nickel, you might say,
Two for a dime if it's
A grandma who's known
Steak and roses in her time.
Play it up. Backhand
Your nose, shiver like a leaf,
And look down at shoes
That were once cows at
The turn of the century.
A hard grandma? Then
Call the dog to roll over,
Whine, and raise a paw.
If the grandma is still
With hands on hips
And shaking her head,
Then call on the dog
To speak a few words
On his back—tiny feet
Prancing in the air.
Make sure it's Sunday
When God is looking around
For something to do.

ODE TO THE YARD SALE

A toaster,
A plate
Of pennies,
A plastic rose
Staring up
To the sky.
It's Saturday
And two friends,
Merchants of
The salvageable heart,
Are throwing
Things onto
The front lawn—
A couch,
A beanbag,
A table to clip
Poodles on,
Drawers of
Potato mashers,
Spoons, knives
That signaled
To the moon
For help.
Rent is due.
It's somewhere
On this lawn,
Somewhere among
The shirts we've
Looked good in,

Taken off before
We snuggled up
To breasts
That almost made
Us gods.
It'll be a good
Day, because
There's much
To sell,
And the pitcher
Of water
Blue in the shade,
Clear in the
Light, with
The much-handled
Scotch the color
Of leaves
Falling at our
Shoes, will
Get us through
The afternoon
Rush of old
Ladies, young women
On their way
To becoming nurses,
Bachelors of
The twice-dipped
Tea bag. It's
An eager day:

Wind in the trees,
Laughter of
Children behind
Fences. Surely
People will arrive
With handbags
And wallets,
To open up coffee
Pots and look
In, weigh pans
In each hand,
And prop hats
On their heads
And ask, "How do
I look?" (foolish
To most,
Beautiful to us).
And so they
Come, poking
At the clothes,
Lifting salt
And pepper shakers
For their tiny music,
Thumbing through
Old magazines
For someone
They know,

As we sit with
Our drinks
And grow sad
That the ashtray
Has been sold,
A lamp, a pillow,
The fry pans
That were action
Packed when
We cooked,
Those things
We threw so much
Love on, day
After day,
Sure they would
Mean something
When it came
To this.

THE JUNGLE CAFE

We could wipe away a fly,
Drink, and order that yellow
Thing behind the glass, peach
Or sweet bread. Sunlight
Is catching on a fork,
Toothy wink from a star.
The fan is busy, the waiter is busy,
And today, in this cafe
Of two dollars and fifty
Cents, we're so important
Dogs are shaking our hands.
"Welcome, turistas," they say,
Or might say if they could
Roll their Rs. Where we sit
It's three o'clock, and
Across the room, where
Old men are playing dominos
It's maybe later, it's maybe
Peru under their hats.
There are toads in this place
—sullen guards by the door—
And the bartender is just another
Uncle fooling with the radio.
"A little to the left,"
I shout, and he dials left,
Then right, until it's German
Polkas, accordions by the sea.
The toads move a little.
An old man clicks a domino.
Omar, my gypsy friend, puts in—
"Love is chasing me up my sleeve."
I salute him, he salutes me,

And together we're so drunk
We're making sense. Little
By little, with rum the color
Of a woman's arm, we're seeing things—
One dancer, no two,
Make that three with one chair.
And that man—the old one
Over there—is so blurry
He thinks he's flying.

AMBITION

for two friends

For years our ambition was to eat
Chicken. To sit in a backyard,
In an after shock of heat
When the sun was out of the way.
This happened. Drunk under a tree
We became sophisticates of the lawn chair
And beer bottles—trumpets we raised
All night under those bitter stars
That turned us to our lies
Of women, lost and found door to door.
"I was lonely once," I told them
And they booed and flicked beer tops
At me—told me to get into
The kitchen for the hard stuff.
When I returned, Chris the failed
Scholar of three degrees
Talked Italy. Flames broke
From the hibachi. The chicken
Grew noisy as a Latin mob.
"Quiet," Jon yelled, and poked them
With a fork onto the platter.
We went inside to argue over salad
—a gaudy hat we stuffed into our mouths—
And let food climb our elbows.
Dogs snapped at bones, whined, jumped
When we threw them buttered rolls,
Corn, rings of potato. We ate
Like Romans with good jobs
And returned to the backyard
To find that the moon had moved
Our chairs. Lost them in fact.
We dropped on the grass, on elbows.

The moon was clearing the trees
By two fingers. I took bets
We'd be happy. "No one ever knows,"
The scholar sighed, empty trumpet
In hand. I smiled. Jon smiled.
Cats with full lives grinned
From the back fence. Sniffed.
Dropped to the ground to nudge us for
The love of chicken but love all the same.

SUNDAY WITHOUT CLOUDS

Today we're hung over
In folding chairs, the TV on
And throwing light at our faces.
It doesn't help. We're dull
As glass kicked around by the sea,
And if someone were to ask
About the sea, we wouldn't know.
All we know is Mexican
Boxing—featherweights
Glistening in the 9th round.
Chris looks at me; I stare at
His chest, for his eyes
Must be blinding. I say
To his chest, "They don't know
What pain is." He brings
A glass of water to his face—
Or what might be his face if I looked.
I get up. At the front window
A lawnful of birds sparring
Over a leaf. A blue sky.
A red thing in the bush.
Above the trees, two clouds with little
Rain to release us from our misery—
The door that keeps slamming
In our heads. Down
The street, not the hint of snow
Or God to end it all,
So we can wake up
And start over again.

THE ESTONIAN COMES TO DINNER

Again I dream the frying pan
Is endless, the tomatoes fat,
The cheese blunt as women on barstools.
I am yours. I take you
To my mouth, the suggestive
Radish at hand, the celery
Clutched like a microphone.
I speak, and important people take note.
I say there's nothing more,
This plate and abused napkin, that wine
Whose memory is deeper than mine.
Estonian, let's show off tonight,
And suck these bones dry, into
Fine slivers that will give off light.
When we eat, let panic rule.
Let cop cars circle the block
And dogs turn on their leashes, crying.
Far off, in the countryside,
Let the cows go to their knees
And hens flutter like books
Thrown from speeding cars.
But we're not going anywhere.
The table is here. The pear that
Was once rain is at hand.
The bread is at hand—the butter,
The potato baked twice
And poked with many eyes.
Let the day end and us begin,
The fork, the knife, the plate all useless.

KEARNEY PARK

True Mexicans or not, let's open our shirts
And dance, a spark of heels
Chipping at the dusty cement. The people
Are shiny like the sea, turning
To the clockwork of rancheras,
The accordion wheezing, the drum-tap
Of work rising and falling.
Let's dance with our hats in hand.
The sun is behind the trees,
Behind my stutter of awkward steps
With a woman who is a brilliant arc of smiles,
An armful of falling water. Her skirt
Opens and closes. My arms
Know no better but to flop
On their own, and we spin, dip
And laugh into each other's faces—
Faces that could be famous
On the coffee table of my abuelita.
But grandma is here, at the park, with a beer
At her feet, clapping
And shouting, "Dance, hijo, dance!"
Laughing, I bend, slide, and throw up
A great cloud of dust,
Until the girl and I are no more.

MORNING ON THIS STREET

It's Saturday with the gray
Noise of rain at the window,
Its fingers weeping to get in.
We're in bunk beds, one brother
Talking football, another
Turning to the dreamed girl
He'd jump from a tree to die for.
Later, in the kitchen,
He tells me, Love is like snow
Or something. I listen
With a bowl at the stove, dress,
And go outside to trees dripping
Rain, a pickup idling
With its headlights on.
I look for something to do
Slowly with a stick
In the absence of love,
That Catholic skirt in a pew.
I walk banging fences
Until Earl the Cartman rattles
Onto our block—a rope over
His shoulder. He pulls hard
Because his wife, centered
On that cart, is cold
Under the rough temple
Of cardboard he's cut for her.
Her legs are bundled in strips
Of white cloth, half there
With the dead, half with us
Who have oranges to give,

As he steps heavily toward
The trees they'll call
Home—a small fire and the black
Haunt of smoke. It's for his wife
That he lives and pulls a rope
To its frayed end. The sky
Is nothing and these neighbors
Wincing behind windows
Are even less. This is marriage,
A man and a woman, in one kind of weather.

TWO

ENVYING THE CHILDREN
OF SAN FRANCISCO

At a city square
Children laugh in the red
Sweaters of Catholics,
As they walk home between trucks
And sunlight angled off buildings that end in points.
I'm holding an apple, among shoppers
Clutching bags big enough to sleep in,
And the air is warm for October—
Torn pieces of paper
Scuttling like roaches, a burst at a time.

The children are blond,
Shiny, and careful at the lights—
The sister with her brother's hand.
They cross looking
At their watches, and I cross too.
I want to know where
They're going, what door they'll push
Open and call home—
The TV coming on,
Milk, a cookie for each hand.

As a kid I wanted to live
In the city, in a building that rose above it all,
The gray streets burst open, a rattle
Of jackhammers. I wanted to
Stare down from the eighteenth floor, and let things go—
My homework for one, a paper plane
With a half-drawn heart and a girl's name.
I wanted to say that I ate
And slept, ate and slept in a building
That faced other buildings, a sliver of sea
Blue in the distance.

I wanted to hear voices
Behind walls, the *click-click* of a poodle
Strolling to his bowl—a violin like fingers
Running down a blackboard.
I wanted to warm my hands at a teakettle
And comb my hair in an elevator, my mouth
Still rolling with cereal, as I started off
For school, a row of pens in my shirt pocket.
Back home at the window
I wanted it to be December—
Flags and honking cars,
A Santa Claus with his pot, a single red
Balloon let go and racing skyward,
And the tiny mothers who would come around
Buildings, disappear, and come around again,
Hugging bags for all they were worth to children.

WHERE WE COULD GO

Happy that this is another
Country, we're going to
Sit before coffees and croissants
On Rue Lucerne
And watch the working fathers
Labor up the street,
A stiff loaf of bread
In each roughed-up hand.
Some nod to us;
Others pass with the moist eyes
Of a strict wind.
This is France, daughter.
This is the autumn of calendars.
The sparrows are like
Those back home fighting
With the lawn,
Squealing and transparent
As their hunger.
They play at our feet,
Then climb to our knees
To hop like windup toys,
Until they're on the table
That's scratched with more
History than either of us—
Their beaks tap for crumbs.
But the waiter shoos them
With a dish towel.
This is a cafe for people,
Not birds, he says,
And so we leave because
We're like birds,

Transparent at love and deceit.
We hunger; we open our mouths . . .
We walk up the street, our shoes
Ringing against the stones,
To stare into a store window —
Clocks, coffee pots, an accordion
Longing for the sea.
But we're miles from the sea.
There are no boats or salt
Climbing our arms.
This is a country town,
And straw is what makes things
Go here — or so says our guidebook.
And it says that there
Is a church, lit with gold
And rare paintings,
And we start off
Hand in hand, smiling
For no reason other than
Everything is new —
The stone buildings, straw
Whacked into bundles.
What's that? my daughter
Asks, and there's no greater
Pleasure than saying,
Beats me. Let's go see.

AUTUMN WITH A DAUGHTER
WHO'S JUST CATCHING ON

You were going to wear red,
Me blue-green, instead we went
To the park in browns. It's easy
To fool the sparrows in such
Colors, if there's bread to
Saucer under gaunt trees.
And that's what we did. The birds
Dropped hints at our feet
And stared at our hands.
They had no idea we were the ones
Who had cut through mountains
And done in the sea,
That we had roughed up rocks
And bruised the sky with smoke.
They hopped in grass; they poked
At leaves and beat their wings
In the dust. Not knowing us,
They made noises so we might love
Them, and toss more than bread.

FAILING IN THE PRESENCE OF ANTS

We live to some purpose, daughter.
Across the park, among
The trees that give the eye
Something to do, let's spread
A blanket on the ground
And examine the ants, loose
Thread to an old coat.
Perhaps they are more human than we are.
They live for the female,
Rescue their hurt, and fall earthward
For their small cause. And
Us? We live for our bellies,
The big O of our mouths.
Give me, give me, they say,
And many people, whole countries,
May go under because we desire TV
And chilled drinks, clothes
That hang well on our bodies—
Desire sofas and angled lamps,
Hair the sea may envy
On a slow day.
It is hurtful to sweep
Ants into a frenzy, blow
Chemicals into their eyes—
Those austere marchers who will lift
Their heads to rumor—seed,
Wafer of leaf, dropped apple—
And start off, over this
And that, between sloppy feet
And staggered chairs, for no
Purpose other than it might be good.

HUNGER AMONG CRABS

I've been translated into three languages
And still I don't make sense
—or so says my daughter, dragging
Her blanket from my arms, her wingless
Shoulders sobbing because I have shouted *No!*
OK I don't make sense, so on a whim
Let's drive across the Bay
Past the throw of lights they call The City,
Beyond the dark industry of sax and smooth guitar.
The sea is there. The gulls
Ride princely, between three-cornered waves.
A man hunches to his cigarette
In the cold, a fishing pole at his feet.
If we were to call him,
He might be an uncle, Japanese or Mexican,
Loose in the same jacket of four beers.
But it's this way, daughter, toward the beached
Seaweed and its last knot. It's the way
To rocks and an arena of crabs, widening.
I'm hungry; you're hungry—and it doesn't make sense.
The crabs march willingly from the sea
To become food, ugly
Against the sand, beautiful to the mouth
That is always open but just now laughing.

UNDER TREES

Like everyone, I'm unsure
Without friends, young
Or old, and I'm all wrong
Even on this street
That is like any other,
With cars and people
And shrubs doing very little
In wind. Love is a way out,
Like a star through the icy trees,
And I may find myself there
Under trees—a woman
With me and living up
To my hands. *Cuerpo a tu cuerpo,*
I could say. *Tus pechos bajo mis ojos.*
We'll be close, even in our faces,
So close that if you looked away
I'd know what you see.

DESIRE

It's easy to hunger.
One day, a night,
And there you are,
Sunlight between fingers,
And looking in
Trees. Birds are
Striking fruit,
An almond open
Like a woman's love,
And a single feather
Rocks downward in air.
You're hungry now.
The tree is quiet—
The nests gone cold,
Birds turn toward fall,
That gray line of
Sparrows and little else.
But it's the fruit
You want—the almond
And its wooden bell,
Plum or cherry,
A fig to push a thumb
Into and part slowly:
The meat wet, dark
Before it's pink,
Its sighs coming
From another mouth.

SHOPPING FOR A WOMAN

Shopping for my wife, I'm lost
To the shrug of skirts, taut calves,
The hair coming up with wind—these women
With their arms hurting for one more red gift.
OK, I admit it. I'm the Catholic
In the lingerie department
Tapping slippers against my palm
And weighing nighties that are sheer as clouds,
Upfront and eager to crumble in my hands.
I buy the cloud, and on the next floor,
A woman behind a counter with
Patou, Givenchy, L'Aire du Temps
Under my nose, splashed on my wrist.
Her throat is open, eyes arched like birds,
And the dark behind her ear is a channel
To the heart. I ask, Is this what women
Want? She lifts her eyes to me
And the birds are gone: her face is fawn-colored,
Quiet in her study of me. Sometimes,
She says, and looks aside to a tray
Of jewelry—pearl necklace,
Earrings showing light. These things too,
She says. And this chain, in gold.

SEEING A GIRL,
GOING HOME TO FIND A BROTHER

For a full day she was a good girl
In her skirt, legs crossed
On her mother's couch, with tea
Steaming from a white cup.
Books, we talked, movies in black
And white—Brando in a T-shirt
And Heddren with her hair full
Of impossible birds. We walked
To the Legion of Honor, a wedge of
Sea far off, and returned to
The apartment, still polite,
Still talking books and movies.
The stove turned blue again
For more tea—evening traffic
In a window, the hiss of
Tires in a light rain. One
More book said, and that shelf
In the brain would be empty,
Be a finger of dust. I touched
Her sleeve, a coy button,
Her blouse shadowed
By my hands. "No please,"
She said, and offered more tea,
Dead literature by memory.
When I reached for a knee, she said
This is the door, that is the street.
Up the street, wind jumped up
And down in my hair all the way
To my brother's place—brother
On a beanbag, Indian-style,
Making noises with a guitar.

I made heavy footsteps,
From window to window—couples
In the same rain, some hand
In hand, others like doves
On a line—close but not
Touching. "Love is nothing
But friction," I said
And went into the kitchen for beers,
Lanterns we hung on our faces
Grins big as hooks to
Throw hats on and say we're home.

THE NEW MOVIES

Friendship is possible.
He's studied that young woman
On the bench, her jaw and the lick
Of hair that falls over her eyes.
She is reading a book, a bitten apple   5
At her side, and it's his task
To greet her, to talk small talk,
Then large issues, like whales,
Until her hand is in his,
And they're off to a museum and then coffee,   10
A foreign movie they don't get.
There is late dinner, a flush
Of wine, and his right hand
Like a badge on her blouse.
They're on the couch, then the floor,   15
The tongue taking its place behind an ear.

After it's over they stare
Into the fire that's gone down,
The smoke of two drinks
Behind their eyes.   20
They talk about artichokes,
Then beets, cucumbers, sprouts . . .
They talk about clouds
Seen from jets, until their talk
Stalls like a cloud. It's 2 A.M.
He pats her hip, smiling.   25
There's little to say
Now that they've come this far.
She steps into her skirt,

He into his pants. The room fills
With the sounds of things closing,   30
Buckles and snaps, buttons
And earrings, zippers that yawn
On the floor but grit their teeth
When they close to say good-bye.

PEPPER TREE

We tapped you into a snug hole,
Staked you to a piece
Of lumber that was once the house,
A rail from the back porch;
That, too, was a tree, cut,
Milled, and slapped with wire
For shipment, back in the thirties.
Don't worry. You're not
Going anywhere, hatrack. The wind
Comes, the sparrows come—
The rain pointless against
Your branches, notched
With a promise of leaves.
You are here, under rain
And the rain of *Get Big*, from my child.

The truth is I don't care
For the street, the banged
Cars and three-legged dogs,
The scuttle of bags
Blowing from the grocery, Lucky Day.
I don't care for the billboard,
The wires crossing and recrossing.
From the front window
I want to look at you,
Green and moving like the sea
In wind. I want you to grow
Heavy with sparrows, and if
A gull has an off day
In the weary sky, let
Your branches bear its screams,

The scraping beak. Let its wings
Open on sores, shoulders hunch,
And eyes stare me back to church.
Under this weight, that color,
Stand up, bend a little, be here tomorrow.

WHEN WE WAKE

Sometimes it's only the square light
Of window, white behind the bushes,
Yellow if it faces the street, in autumn.
Sometimes it's a young woman with a book
In her mittened hand,
Off to work, a lover's house perhaps.
I cross the street
With my own book, with my own gloves:
I note a strand of hair from under her beret,
The eyes, her face flushed from
The rain we walk against in any weather.
Sometimes it's a grandfather on a bench,
Legs crossed, hands fiddling
In his sweater pocket—
His face is happy, now worried, now happy again.
For years I have been asleep
But now I am awake to this life. The trees
Lowered across an indifferent sea,
Failing at the shore. I sat
With my eyes closed on a landscape

Of childhood—a chinaberry, the broken
Glass that gritted its many teeth
All summer. Now I am awake.
This city is filled with people with hats
In their hands or on their knees,
And I am amazed that I missed them—
Amazed at the women stepping onto
Buses, their calf muscles taut,
Their purses creaking with goods.
There are children, a waitress in a yellow
Apron, my neighbor bending down

To a tulip in the yard. I could approach
Any one of them with simple questions:
Is this Tuesday? Are pears in season?
If they said *yes* or *no* or *maybe*,
If the dog made a noise, if the weather stayed
Where it was, it could be a start.
The cat is in the sun, the sun in the trees,
The trees against a blue to remember . . .

SEEING THINGS

To a cow we could be bushes
On the run. To a cat
A warm place behind a hand.
We're odd light. Today
I saw you as noise
In my arms, legs pumping
And face red enough
To warm a cold room.
Strange that we should leave
The table—carrots, an apple
Quartered and rocking
In your dish—
And when I pointed out
The hills from the balcony
That you should start
Your machinery, the tears
And tiny fists,
The crying like rope
Going taut. When this
Happened, I went inside
To calm down and remember
The sparrows that would
Hop in snow that they might live
At our windows, in spring.
Inside I poured wine
Until the room saddened
And went back outside—
The hills lit with homes
In the early dusk.
You didn't cry. You raised
A hand to a leaf, smoke
From a chimney,

And tugged my beard
That we should go inside?
We went inside, played
On the rug before
You looked at a chair
And started up your machinery,
Its wheel picking up
Speed when I showed you
A picture on the wall.
Daughter, I thought,
What starts laughter,
Squeals, a happy mouth?
You tore at my hair,
Tears leaping like seed,
And it wasn't me.

SATURDAY UNDER THE SKY

This morning, with the rain tapping
The shoulders of everyone we will ever love—
Your mother for one, those dogs
Trotting for leaves—
We could go to the aquarium—
Angel fish and eels, the gray plop
Of toads among rocks. We
Could walk slowly, with a balloon
Banging against my head,
Walk with other fathers and
Daughters tapping the glass cases
For the lizard to waken
And the snake roll from
One dried limb to the next. We
Could handle a starfish, lift
A spiny thing, green in the water,
Blue in our hands. Instead
It's the Hall of Science
Where we stand before mirrors
That stretch us tall, then squeeze us
Squat as suitcases bound for Chicago.
There are rocks, the strata
Of earth, a black cut of oil far down.
There are computers, a maze of lights
And wires, steel balls bouncing
About—they could be us, if we should make
The moon one day. But you tire
In a room mixed up with stars
And it's juice and a pretzel
On the bench, with me thinking
I'm a good father. When we leave
Rain is still tapping shoulders
With everyone looking around,

Hunched in their coats.
The wind picks at the trees,
At the shrubs. The sky rolls and
The balloon tied to your wrist is banging
Unfairly against my head: *What else! What else!*

EATING BREAD

The days are filled with air. A cloud
Over a tree. A thud of mail
In the box, and the steps of our carrier
Descending the porch. Someone is thinking
Of us, right now in the improbable heart,
And it must be good: you've chewed a smile
In your bread. "Look," you say, and I look.
I chew a smile, and press it to yours.
This is what we need. A slice
Of bread, a little quiet,
A window to sit before with our mouths full—
The neighbor kids at baseball,
A dog, that girl who could be your sister
Peeling an orange at the curb.

Daughter, though we smile with bread,
I'm troubled at not knowing what tugs the soul,
God or love, women or love,
And at how we can live in this world
With the dead itching on their racks,
A country in flames, the poor
Crouching before their banged-up bowls.
How can I tell you this? How can I show
You the men who want to hurt us all the way
To the grave. You with the hands,
The tiny teeth, the eyes that could save us
From ourselves, as right now.
You point to a bird, say "bird,"
And it lifts from a wire to a branch.
You wave, and the kids drop their gloves
To wave back. A dog looks up, a paper cup
In his mouth. Little one, tell me how this happens.

FINDING A LUCKY NUMBER

to a nephew

When I was like you I crossed a street
To a store, and from the store
Up an alley, as I rolled chocolate
In my mouth and looked around
With my face. The day was blue
Between trees, even without wind,
And the fences were steaming
And a dog was staring into a paint bucket
And a Mexicano was raking
Spilled garbage into a box,
A raffle of eggshells and orange peels.
He nodded his head and I nodded mine
And rolled chocolate all the way
To the courthouse, where I sat
In the park, with a leaf falling
For every person who passed—
Three leaves and three daughters
With bags in their hands.
I followed them under trees,
The leaves rocking out of reach
Like those skirts I would love
From a distance. I lost them
When I bent down to tie my shoes
And begged a squirrel to eat grass.
Looking up, a dog on the run,
A grandma with a cart,
And Italians clicking dominoes
At a picnic table—men
Of the old world, in suits big enough
For Europe. I approached
Them like a squirrel, a tree
At a time, and when I was close
Enough to tell the hour from their wrists,

One laughed with hands in his hair
And turned to ask my age.
"Twelve," I said, and he knocked
My head softly with a knuckle:
"Lucky number, Sonny." He bared
His teeth, yellow and crooked
As dominoes, and tapped the front ones
With a finger. "I got twelve—see."
He opened wide until his eyes were lost
In the pouches of fat cheeks,
And I, not knowing what to do, looked in.

TEACHING NUMBERS

The moon is one,
The early stars a few more . . .
The sycamore is lean
With sparrows, four perhaps,
Three hunched like hoods
And one by itself,
Wiping a beak
In the rag of its shoulder.

From where we sit
We could count to a thousand
By pointing at oranges
On trees, bright lanterns
Against the dusk, globes
Of water that won't come down.

Follow me with this, then:
A stray on two legs
At a trash can, one kite in a tree,
And a couple with four hands,
Three in pockets and one scratching
An ear busy with sound:
Door, cat, scrambling leaf.

(The world understands numbers—
At birth, you're not much
And when lowered into the earth
You're even less, a broken
Toy of 108 bones and 23 teeth
That won't stop laughing.)

But no talk of this
For the dog is happy with an eggshell
And oranges are doing wonders
At this hour in the trees
And there is popcorn to pick
From my small bowl of hands.

Let's start again,
With numbers that will help.

The moon is one,
The early stars a few more . . .

THESE DAYS

In my dreams
A child is crying into a steering wheel
And Omar is holding onto a tree
And a shot horse is staring me into the next room.

That was last night, and the night before.
Today the two of us walked
In a park—cruel place
With pigeons bickering
Over spewed popcorn.

Later I heard on the radio—
A plane on the water,
And the gulls pecking the dead into greater number.

Or so I imagined.
And so it might be
Because it's all possible—
The dead with wind in their hair,
Another war, the half-lid
Of sun going down
In dust.

This scares me.
If we go up in ash we come down as ash.
And what are we then?
A dark crescent under a fingernail,
A smudge in the air?

Believe me, daughter,
I want to say something true,
That we will get up on time,
That I'll have coffee and you an egg,
Yellow sun on a plate.

But I can't even say this.
The world is mad.
Dying things show up behind doors.
Soldiers toss severed feet for the TV.

Little one, stay where you are.
Hold hands, and don't let go.

IN STORM

Rain or no rain, let's admit it's Tuesday,
That apples are not enough,
That I'm tired of horse
And dog, the toppling thrones of blocks.
Daughter, the yard is open to suggestion.
Leaves are there, and under them,
Snails in their journey to become the sea.
Emptied, they will blow
In wind, without the clouds moving on.
There is the woodpile,
The grass and the four o'clocks showing through.
There is the pumpkin, dented
With rot. If I opened it
With a shovel it would rush
Seeds, wet as teared eyes, into your hands—
Hands that point, grasp, poke . . .
Daughter, everything is here
For your first memory, the sparrows
And cat, the lemon swelling bright
Against the turned leaves.
If you ran on the grass, you might slip
And come up wet, perhaps crying.
This could be important,
An image to turn over all the way to the end.
Take a step. Learn something.

HOW THINGS WORK

Today it's going to cost us twenty dollars
To live. Five for a softball. Four for a book,
A handful of ones for coffee and two sweet rolls,
Bus fare, rosin for your mother's violin.
We're completing our task. The tip I left
For the waitress filters down
Like rain, wetting the new roots of a child
Perhaps, a belligerent cat that won't let go
Of a balled sock until there's chicken to eat.
As far as I can tell, daughter, it works like this:
You buy bread from a grocery, a bag of apples
From a fruit stand, and what coins
Are passed on helps others buy pencils, glue,
Tickets to a movie in which laughter
Is thrown into their faces.
If we buy a goldfish, someone tries on a hat.
If we buy crayons, someone walks home with a broom.
A tip, a small purchase here and there,
And things just keep going. I guess.

SMALL FOREST

Honey, when we get there
Inside the trees,
We could walk
With sticks and look
Like real hikers
With a knapsack choked
With this and that,
A canteen banging
Our waists—or we
Could grunt up a hill,
Look left, look right,
And leap a stream,
Land in the stream,
But think it's OK,
Because to be wet
Is to be alive,
Which is why we're here
On our first stop,
With the ocean
Up the road,
And Mariko, steps behind,
Whining like a tire
That she wants
Some snakes, a lion,
Wolf, the lake
I promised, and,
Daddy please, why
Don't we get in the car
And be over there.

THE TREES THAT CHANGE OUR LIVES

When I was twenty I walked past
The lady I would marry—
Cross-legged on the porch.
She was cracking walnuts
With a hammer, a jar
At her side. I had come
From the store, swinging
A carton of cold beers,
And when I looked she smiled.
And that was all, until
I came back, flushed,
Glowing like a lantern
Against a backdrop
Of silly one-liners—
Cute-face, peaches, baby-lips.

We talked rain, cats,
About rain on cats,
And later went inside
For a sandwich, a glass
Of milk, sweets.
Still later, a month later,
We were going at one
Another on the couch, bed,
In the bathtub
And its backwash of bubbles,
Snapping. So it went,
And how strangely: the walnut
Tree had dropped its hard
Fruit, and they, in turn,

Were dropped into a paper
Bag, a jar, then into
The dough that was twisted
Into bread for the love
Of my mouth, so
It might keep talking.

GETTING SERIOUS

I shave my face, comb my hair
Back on the sides, and I'm different
From the posture I assumed in a grunting sleep.
It's time to get serious,
To cough delicately into a soft hand,
To weigh each meal on a fork, not my unbalanced tongue.
I've turned thirty, brighter
By an espresso and paperback translations,
And my task is to be polite:
I hold open a door, and people rush in.
I help my wife with her coat,
And she smiles like a red coal blooming under wind.
So it is. I'm crisp
In slacks, a stiff collar,
And I'm off to witness a French romance.
This will take years. I turn thirty-five,
Still crisp, and the theater is weeping,
Its lap full of popcorn and hands
Petting one another's love so it won't be sad.

LOOKING AROUND, BELIEVING

How strange that we can begin at anytime.
With two feet we get down the street.
With a hand we undo the rose.
With an eye we lift up the peach tree
And hold it up to the wind—white blossoms
At our feet. Like today. I started
In the yard with my daughter,
With my wife poking at a potted geranium,
And now I am walking down the street,
Amazed that the sun is only so high,
Just over the roof, and a child
Is singing through a rolled newspaper
And a terrier is leaping like a flea
And at the bakery I pass, a palm
Like a suctioning starfish, is pressed
To the window. We're keeping busy—
This way, that way, we're making shadows
Where sunlight was, making words
Where there was only noise in the trees.

BETWEEN WORDS

Just what is there to do? Eat
Is one, sleep is another.
But before the night ends
We could walk under
These camphors, hand in hand
If you like, namedropping
The great cities of the past,
And if a dog should join
Us with his happy tail,
The three of us could talk,
Politics perhaps, medicine
If our feet should hurt
For the sea.

      Love,
The moon is between clouds,
And we're between words
That could deepen
But never arrive.
Like this walk. We could go
Under trees and moons,
With the stars tearing
Like mouths in the night sky,
And we'll never arrive.
That's the point. To go
Hand in hand, with the words
A sparrow could bicker
Over, a dog make sense of
Even behind a closed door,
Is what it's about.
A friend says, be happy. Desire.

Remember the blossoms
In rain, because in the end
Not even the ants
Will care who we were
When they climb our faces
To undo the smiles.